THE BABY GOD PROMISED

Luke 1:26—2:20 FOR CHILDREN

Written by Walter Wangerin Jr.

Illustrated by Bill Heuer

MANUFACTURED IN THE UNITED STATES OF AMERICA

ISBN 0-570-06105-9

Publishing House
St. Louis

ARCH Books

Mary had a baby.
Mary had a baby.
She named her baby Jesus.
She knew the babe would ease us.
Ah, Mary had a baby boy,
And this is the way that it was.

The angel named Gabriel strolled in her yard
And told her to sit and be still.
"You're special," he said, "in the eyes of the
Lord,
Handpicked, after He has been looking so hard
For someone to do His good will.

“Maid, you are the garden of God today,
And in you He is planting His seed.
That seed will grow bigger in every way
Until it is born as a boy who will say
That God is His Father indeed!”

Then Mary was staring at this and at that;
"A baby," she whispered so low.
The angel had left her; but there was the cat;
She had to tell someone, and so she said,
"Cat—
A baby, well what do you know!"

Then Mary was rushing as fast as she could
To tell somebody else the good news:
The baby inside of her had to be good
Since He would be doing what other men should.
Oh, she ran! Oh, she wore out her shoes.

Then whom should she go to? And whom did she find?
Her kin named Elizabeth;
And when she said "Hi!" to this lady so kind,
Elizabeth shouted, "I just had a sign!
I know why you're out of breath."

Elizabeth giggled, she wiggled her toes;
She grinned and showed all of her teeth.
"A babe is inside of you, I would suppose,
The one Heaven promised, the one Heaven chose
To save us from sin and from death!

“Ah, lucky my Mary, and lucky me, too:
You came to *my* kitchen, to *me*!”
And Mary said, “Yes”; she said, “Bessie, that’s true;
Our Lord has been watching the likes of us two,
The lowest there is; but Bessie, we’re *His*,
Then how grand and important are we!”

Ah, Mary had a baby, sweet Mary had a boy;
And Heaven said, "You name your joy
Immanuel: He'll know you well."
Good Mary bore a bouncing boy,
And this is the way that it was.

Now, the king in the capital wanted to know
How many his citizens were.
"My people, you pack your baggage and go
To the towns of your mammas and papas,
    and so
I will count you by families there."

Then the people were traveling thither
    and yon—
Grumbling as they passed through the streets;
They shoved and they bustled until they were
    done;
They fussed and they hustled to be the first
    one
To find a hotel with clean sheets.

But Mary moved slowly; round Mary rode
slow;
She couldn't go faster than that.
See, the baby inside of her—how He did grow!
He was big; He was ready to come, don't you
know.
So when Mary was tired, she sat.

But Joseph was with her; her husband was
there,
And he was the kindest of men:
He brought her her water, and he didn't care
If they were the last ones to find the last chair
In the last room in Bethlehem.

Now Mary is groaning, and Joseph is knocking
On every dark door in the night;
But all he can hear is citizens locking
Their doors and their porches. Oh, what is
    more shocking
Than Mary alone and no light?

Poor Mary is groaning: There isn't much
    time;
Her baby is coming so soon.
And Joseph is sweating as bright as a dime,
But "Never mind me," he calls; "I'll help
    you climb
To the stall that I found for a room."

The baby! The baby! Oh, Mary, have your
Savior.
Dear Mary, bear your boy.
You give Him birth, and men on earth
Shall call Him Christ, Messiah, Worth;
They'll look at each other with joy.

The shepherds are playing at mumblety-peg
For something to do to keep warm,
Are tired and griping with pains in the leg,
And one of them shouting, "Who gobbled
my egg?
The shepherd who did that, I'll shatter his
arm!"
These herders know nothing but harm.

Then shepherd and shepherd is hiding his
head
In his coat like a Halloween hood;
They huddle together like sheep full of dread;
They fear that the weather will soon strike
them dead—
For a light in the night means no good.

But *this* light is speaking; and this light
is glory;
For this is an angel on earth.
"Look up," he implores, "and I'll tell you
a story
More happy than any that you've heard before
me.
Shepherds, there's just been a birth!

"Jesus, the Savior, your Christ and your Lord
Has been born on this night, this good night!
He waits in a manger; His pillow's a board;
His clothes are but bunting, BUT HE IS
YOUR LORD!"
Then millions of angels are everywhere
soaring,
And here and there, everywhere, angels are
roaring
That God in His glory, that God is now
pouring
His peace on mankind and His might!

Hush Shepherds, be quiet. Oh, Shepherds, be
still;
The night is a calm one again.
You stare at each other, you stare at the hill
Where the angels were singing. You know
God's good will:
Get up. Go to Bethlehem.

And there is His father, and there is His mother,
And there is the baby, the boy.
And here are the shepherds in love with each other,
For what are they now? They are brother and brother
Because of this baby, their joy.

So Mary had a baby
And Mary bore a brilliant child.
His name is Most High; and because of Him I,
And heaven, and everyone smiled.

DEAR PARENTS:

This retelling of the Christmas story emphasizes the gradually growing ripples of light that our Lord's birth brought with it. Christ comes to earth as a seed of light planted in Mary's womb and grows to the "brilliant child" who enlightens the face of heaven itself, and causes us all to smile.

At the same time, the amazing ordinariness of the events is emphasized. Jesus came into the lives of real people, not just of characters in somebody's myth. So the narration combines the two elements of the incarnation: the glory of the Lord and the human situation that glory entered.

Help your child discover all the ordinary things in the story, e. g., Elizabeth's teeth, Mary's cat, Joseph's sweaty face as shiny as a dime. Then trace through the story what we might call our sinful situation, e. g., the crowds, the pain, the tired, griping shepherds, etc. Finally, discover with your children how the light Jesus brought gradually grows from a little seed to the great light of the angels in the sky to the glorious radiance of our redemption.

Perhaps you can summarize with something like, "At Christmas Jesus came from heaven into our world and brought with Him His beautiful smile so that now we all can smile too."

THE EDITOR